Georgia, My State
Geographic Regions

Appalachian Plateau

by Doraine Bennett

STATE
STANDARDS
PUBLISHING®

Your State • Your Standards • Your Grade Level

Dear Educators, Librarians and Parents ...

Thank you for choosing the *"Georgia, My State"* Series! We have designed this series to support the Georgia Department of Education's Georgia Performance Standards for elementary level Georgia studies. Each book in the series has been written at appropriate grade level as measured by the ATOS Readability Formula for Books (Accelerated Reader), the Lexile Framework for Reading, and the Fountas & Pinnell Benchmark Assessment System for Guided Reading. Photographs and/or illustrations, captions, and other design elements have been included to provide supportive visual messaging to enhance text comprehension. Glossary and Word Index sections introduce key new words and help young readers develop skills in locating and combining information.

We wish you all success in using the *"Georgia, My State"* Series to meet your student or child's learning needs. For additional sources of information, see www.georgiaencyclopedia.org.

Jill Ward, President

Publisher
State Standards Publishing, LLC
1788 Quail Hollow
Hamilton, GA 31811
USA
1.866.740.3056
www.statestandardspublishing.com

Library of Congress Cataloging-in-Publication Data
Bennett, Doraine, 1953-
  Appalachian Plateau / by Doraine Bennett.
     p. cm. -- (Georgia, my state. Geographic Regions)
  Includes index.
  ISBN-13: 978-1-935077-19-0 (hardcover)
  ISBN-10: 1-935077-19-8 (hardcover)
  ISBN-13: 978-1-935077-24-4 (pbk.)
  ISBN-10: 1-935077-24-4 (pbk.)
  1. Georgia--Juvenile literature. 2. Georgia--Geography--Juvenile literature. I. Title.
  F286.3.B46 2009
  917.58'3--dc22

                              2009013002

Table of Contents

This is the Appalachian Plateau region.

Appalachian Plateau

Blue Ridge

Valley and Ridge

Piedmont

Upper Coastal Plain

Lower Coastal Plain

The Appalachian Plateau is in the northwest corner of Georgia.

Let's Explore!

Hi, I'm Bagster! Let's explore the Appalachian Plateau **geographic region**. A region is an area named for the way the land is formed. The Appalachian Plateau is the smallest geographic region of Georgia. Can you find it on a map? It's in the northwest corner of Georgia.

Mountains in the Appalachian Plateau have flat tops.

What is a Plateau?

Let's go to **Lookout Mountain**. **Sand Mountain** is nearby. Most mountains have tall peaks. These mountains are different. They have flat tops. This high, flat land is called a **plateau**. It is part of the Appalachian Plateau.

Tennessee

Lookout Mountain

← **Appalachian Plateau Region**

Pigeon Mountain

Valley and Ridge Region

Alabama

Where is Lookout Mountain?

Part of Lookout Mountain is in Georgia.

Part of it is in Tennessee. And part of it

is in Alabama.

Cherokee Indians once lived in this region.

Sand Mountain is across the valley from Lookout Mountain.

Cherokee Indians Lived Here

Let's stand on top of Lookout Mountain.

Lookout Valley is to the west. Sand Mountain is across the **valley**. A valley is an area of low land between mountains or hills. Cherokee Indians once lived here. They called the mountain *Chatanuga*. That means *mountains looking at each other*.

They can soar like an eagle!

Fly Like a Bird!

Have you ever wanted to fly? People in **hang gliders** jump from the steep cliffs on Lookout Mountain. A hang glider is like a giant kite that people ride in the air. Strap on your helmet. Climb into the harness. Run, run, run! Jump off the side of the mountain! Soar like an eagle!

Cloudland Canyon is part of Lookout Mountain.

Look deep into the canyon!

What is a Canyon?

Let's look down into **Cloudland Canyon**. It is part of Lookout Mountain. A **canyon** is a deep cut into the earth. Wind and water carve away the soil to make the cut deeper or wider. Walk around the top and look deep into the canyon.

The creek falls over the rocks and makes waterfalls.

It's a long way to the bottom of the canyon!

Climb Down Into the Canyon!

Let's hike to the bottom of Cloudland Canyon. **Sitton Gulch Creek** flows down into the canyon. The trail is steep. Part of the trail is a stone staircase with 600 steps! We will see **waterfalls**. The creek water falls over the rocks into a pool down below. Are your legs tired?

Ellison's Cave is as deep as two football fields!

What is Inside the Mountain?

Let's explore **Ellison's Cave**. A cave is a deep hole in the earth. Ellison's Cave is southeast of Lookout Mountain. It is one of the deepest caves in the United States. One part of the cave drops very deep into the earth. It is as deep as two football fields. Hold on tight!

Some rocks are as large as a house!

Rocks have strange shapes at Rocktown.

Look at Those Strange Shapes!

Erosion makes rocks in the Appalachian Plateau form strange shapes. Erosion happens when water and wind break down the rocks bit by bit. Some of these rocks are as large as a house. Rock climbers like to go to **Rocktown**. Let's go rock climbing!

Glossary

canyon – A deep cut into the earth.

Cloudland Canyon – A large canyon that is part of Lookout Mountain.

Ellison's Cave – A deep hole in the earth near Lookout Mountain. It is one of the deepest caves in the United States.

erosion – What happens to land when wind and water wear away the soil.

geographic region – An area named for the way the land is formed.

hang gliders – Giant kites that people ride in the air.

Lookout Mountain – The largest mountain in the Appalachian Plateau.

Lookout Valley – The low land to the west of Lookout Mountain.

plateau – Land that is high and flat.

Rocktown – A place where people like to climb big rocks. Rocktown was caused by erosion long ago.

Sand Mountain – A large mountain west of Lookout Mountain.

Sitton Gulch Creek – A creek that helped form Cloudland Canyon.

valley – An area of low land that lies between mountains or hills.

waterfalls – Water from a creek or river that falls over the rocks.

Word Index

Image Credits

Cover	Photo courtesy Georgia Department of Economic Development
p.4	Photo courtesy Georgia Department of Economic Development
p.6	Photo courtesy Georgia Department of Economic Development
p.8	Photos courtesy Georgia Department of Economic Development
p.10	valley: © Diane Carr, Columbus, Georgia; Cherokees: Photo courtesy Tennessee State Library and Archives, Nashville, Tennessee
p.12	hang glider: Photo courtesy Georgia Department of Economic Development; small glider: © Diane Carr, Columbus, Georgia
p.14	Cloudland Canyon: © Diane Carr, Columbus, Georgia; father and son: Photo courtesy Georgia Department of Economic Development
p.16	Photos courtesy Georgia Department of Economic Development
p.18	Photos © Willie Hunt
p.20	Photos courtesy Georgia Department of Economic Development

About the Author

Doraine Bennett has a degree in professional writing from Columbus State University in Columbus, Georgia, and has been writing and teaching writing for over twenty years. She has authored numerous articles in magazines for both children and adults and is the editor of the National Infantry Association's *Infantry Bugler* magazine. Doraine enjoys reading and writing books and articles for children. She lives in Georgia with her husband, Cliff.